SHAKESPEARE
in the Garden

SHAKESPEARE *in the* Garden

A Selection of Gardens and an Illustrated Alphabet of Plants

MICK HALES

ABRAMS,
NEW YORK

Project Manager: Margaret Kaplan
Designer: Darilyn Lowe Carnes
Production Manager: Jane Searle

Library of Congress Cataloging-in-Publication Data

Hales, Mick.
  Shakespeare in the garden : a selection of gardens and an alphabet of plants / Mick Hales.
    p. cm.
  Includes bibliographical references and index.
  ISBN-13: 978-0-8109-5716-9 (hardcover : alk. paper)
  ISBN-10: 0-8109-5716-7 (hardcover : alk. paper)
1. Shakespeare, William, 1564-1616—Knowledge—Botany. 2. Gardens—England.
3. Gardens—United States. 4. Gardens—Canada. 5. Gardens in literature.
6. Plants in literature. I. Title.

PR3041.H35 2006
822.3'3—dc22

                            2006003671

Text and photographs © 2006 Mick Hales

Printed and bound in Singapore
10 9 8 7 6 5 4 3 2 1

HNA ▌▌▌▌▌
harry n. abrams, inc.
a subsidiary of La Martinière Groupe
115 West 18th Street
New York, NY 10011
www.hnabooks.com

All photographs are copyright © Mick Hales.
Anne Hathaway's Cottage, Stratford-on-Avon: 11-13;
Ballymaloe Farm, County Cork: 127; Birth Place, Stratford-on-
Avon: 8, 109; Central Park, New York: 36-41; Cranborne Manor,
Dorset: 2-3, 24-31, 110, 130, 141; Generalife, Granada: 98;
Heacham, Norfolk: 1, 82-83; Mayflower Inn, Washington, CT:
50-55; Montgomery, AL: 62-65; New Place, Stratford-on-Avon:
9, 15-17; Northwestern University, Evanston, IL: 57-61;
Private garden, Sussex: 138; Stanley Park, Vancouver, BC: 78-
81; St. Mary's-at-Lambeth, London: 32-35; Stratford Festival,
Stratford, ON: 66-73; University College of the Fraser Valley,
Chilliwack, BC: 75-77; Vassar College, Poughkeepsie, NY: 6,
42-49; Wistmans Wood, Dartmoor, Devon: 118.

Contents

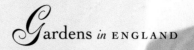
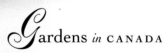

$\mathcal{I}$ntroduction

WILLIAM SHAKESPEARE WAS BORN DURING A TIME OF EXTRAORDINARY FERVOR IN POLITICS, religion, and literary development in England. It was the end of the Tudor era and the beginning of the Jacobean. Coming from the provincial market town of Stratford-on-Avon, in Warwickshire, Shakespeare grew up in a close-knit community. His father, John, was active in Stratford government and a good businessman. William received a classical education in the local grammar school. His careful observation of people and the many facets of humanity, of plants, and the ways of nature, gave him a deep well of insight to draw upon throughout his creative life. His love of nature is revealed in his texts as he draws analogies among feelings, thoughts, the state of the nation, evil and good, and the everyday life of the garden. This has led many to believe that he must have spent time in his mother's garden in Henley Street. And perhaps he observed the countryside as he walked to his girlfriend Anne Hathaway's home in nearby Shottery.

For us in the twenty-first century, it is hard to conceive of life in Shakespeare's time, twenty-five years before Isaac Newton was born. Fairies and pixies were alive in people's minds, especially in country life. Plague after plague swept through England, hitting hard in the larger towns. People were hounded or even killed for their religious beliefs. To be politically incorrect might well mean being thrown into the Tower of London. British theater was in its very infancy and performed mostly in pubs or public squares. It was considered the work of riffraff and was certainly frowned upon by the Puritans. Boys played the parts of women, who were not allowed on stage.

Still, new ideas were flooding in from Renaissance Italy and from elsewhere on the Continent in religion, painting, architecture, and the art of gardening. Many in England dove into this "new age" with their own perspective. Gardening seems always to have been part

Above: Bird bath, Shakespeare Garden, Vassar College.

of the English soul. New ideas about flower gardens, good or bad taste and style in gardens, and the fashion for growing foreign plants flourished throughout English society. Many great minds contemporary with Shakespeare wrote about plants and gardening. Some, like Francis Bacon, John Gerard, Gervase Markham, and John Tradescant the Elder, wrote insightfully on the subject. John Parkinson in his *Paradisi in sole terrestris* expressed the wonderment of the era for nature and creation, stating: "Whoever wants to compare Art with Nature and our parks with Eden, indiscreetly measures the stride of an elephant by the stride of a mite and the flight of an eagle by that of a gnat."

But it was William Shakespeare who breathed the garden into the heart and lives of the many characters he created, giving us a glimpse of how embedded nature was in their daily lives. His gift was to perceive the beauty of the ordinary and not allow it to be overshadowed by the dark side of humanity, to exalt the joys of love and not run from the realities of death, to observe all facets of what we call life and place them before his audience.

Shakespeare in the Garden offers a glimpse of the Bard's love of nature and how he used it to express the life around him. It is not intended to be a scholarly work on Shakespeare, nor indeed a horticultural treatise on plants of his period. It is a book that I hope will help the reader imagine Shakespeare's garden images, its trees and plants. These images were so much a part of the fabric of his life that they are interwoven seamlessly into his plays and sonnets, as this book aims to show by drawing them together as a collection. To set the scene and context, a brief reference accompanies each of the quotations from Shakespeare's texts, explaining who is speaking and what is happening within the play.

The book also looks at "Shakespeare gardens," which are gardens in the Elizabethan style or created with plants about which he wrote. These gardens are a result of the sheer love people have for Shakespeare's writing on nature and are a way to commemorate his gift to us all, hundreds of years later. Many were planted as a commemoration of his birth or death. The term "Shakespeare garden" is relatively loose, and it is really up to the gardener to determine what the guidelines will be and how strictly to adhere to Elizabethan garden style or Shakespeare's plants in varieties true to his time. Many of the plants are not hardy enough to be grown outside the English climate, and many are difficult to find in their original varieties. The essence of a Shakespeare garden is to reflect with things natural the full range of human life: the passing of beauty with a rose; middle age with the flowers of midsummer; the tragic state of the nation with an untended garden; the color of a bad orange for the blush of an unfaithful maid. The possibilities are endless, just as Shakespeare's writing seems to be—the more you turn it over, the more it grows.

Stratford-on-Avon, WARWICKSHIRE, ENGLAND

THE THREE HOUSES MOST ASSOCIATED WITH SHAKESPEARE'S LIFE IN STRATFORD-ON-AVON ARE his birthplace, the Henley Street home of his parents, John and Mary; his wife Anne Hathaway's cottage; and New Place, the house he bought when his playwriting had earned him good money. Today, his birthplace and Anne Hathaway's cottage still exist in close likeness to Elizabethan times, but New Place was leveled to the ground by the eccentric Reverend Francis Gastrell. This was the last act in his escalating feud with visitors wishing to see Shakespeare's old home and the mulberry tree that is believed to have been a gift of James I. In 1759, Gastrell destroyed the tree in a fit of anger. Later, he left town for a period, triggering a land tax that he refused to pay. He tore down the house to spite the City Council and was run out of Stratford, never to return. No one with that surname was allowed to live there again.

Shakespeare was born in April of 1564 and was lucky to survive childhood. His two older sisters died as infants when the bubonic plague swept through Stratford, killing 15 percent of the population. His father was a successful businessman and glove-maker, and what is now called Shakespeare's Birth Place was a prosperous house set in the heart of Stratford.

The gardens at Birth Place were probably quite functional, growing herbs, fruits, and vegetables. Today, a line of holly trees divides the garden in two. On one side, a lawn allows the many visitors some breathing space, on the other there is a double border of country flowers such as poppies, roses, asters, daisies, ferns, goldenrod, and hollyhocks. Against a boxwood backdrop are a series of herbs including sorrel, hyssop, perennial camomile, winter savory, comfrey, germander, and sweet marjoram. There are solid beds of violas close to the house and climbing roses scale the oak beams. Medlars, crab apples, and oak trees add to the Shakespearean plantings.

Opposite: A mixed border at Birth Place.
Above: An herb garden at the original site of New Place.

As William grew older, he started courting Anne Hathaway in the nearby village of Shottery, about a mile's walk from his home in Henley Street. The Hathaways were yeoman farmers, freeholders of a lower status than gentlemen, but still relatively well off. They lived at Newlands Farm (now known as Anne Hathaway's Cottage), and had ninety acres. Anne's father, Richard, had married twice, and there were eight children in the household. At eighteen, William was successful in courting Anne, eight years his senior. Anne became pregnant and they married hastily, in November 1582, before their daughter Susanna was born. After the marriage the couple lived with William's family on Henley Street. Twins, Hamnet and Judith, were born to them in February 1585. It must have seemed that William's future was bound to Stratford, working in his father's business, but William had itchy feet and too much creative force in him. His heart was with the wandering theaters and actors who came down from London. In about 1587, he went to London to follow his passion for the theater, leaving his family with his parents.

Today, Anne Hathaway's Cottage has a bright, quintessential cottage garden in front of it, with an herb-and-vegetable garden alongside leading to an orchard. The garden is gay with the colors of poppies, lupines, roses, daisies, lady's bonnets, bachelor buttons, chives, sorrel, cardoons, leaf beet, rhubarb chard, crimson broad beans, and gooseberries. The thatched cottage is of two periods and levels (the lower being from the 1460s and the higher from the 1600s) and, despite a fire in the 1960s, is essentially as it was in Anne's time. A tree garden was planted on the property in 1988, with some forty varieties that Shakespeare mentions. An interesting feature in the orchard is a willow cabin whose interwoven branches create a living shelter. It encloses a wooden bench wired to deliver Shakespeare sonnets to the visitor; it was inspired by Viola's speech in Twelfth Night, Act 1, Scene 5, Line 257:

> Make me a willow cabin at your gate
> And call upon my soul within the house,
> Write loyal cantons of contemnèd love,
> And sing them loud even in the dead of night . . .

William's early years in London coincided with great events in English history. In 1587, Queen Elizabeth ordered the execution of Mary, Queen of Scots. In 1588, Philip II of Spain's Armada was defeated, and although the war with Spain lasted twenty years, there was a flowering in commerce and the arts, especially in the theater, with many new playwrights coming out of the universities of Oxford and Cambridge. William was immersed in this cauldron of activity, slowly building his reputation as an actor and writer. Whenever there was a plague, the theaters had to close, and often the company would then travel into the countryside to perform in

Anne Hathaway's Cottage.

Left: The vegetable garden and apple orchard at Anne Hathaway's Cottage.

Above: A cabin made with interwoven willows sits beside the orchard in Ann Hathaway's garden.

various towns. In the summer of 1592, a plague struck that persisted through 1593, and it is thought that William returned to his family in Stratford during this time to write.

It was a difficult time in Stratford. Because of consecutive droughts, there was little food. Two devastating fires in the town left many homeless and necessitated the pulling down of one end of the Henley Street house to prevent it from catching fire. In the summer of 1596, William returned from London at the death of his only son, Hamnet. The next year William had enough money to buy New Place, the second-largest building in Stratford and the only one built of brick. It came complete with two barns, two gardens, and two orchards. This was the first house he owned and it needed quite a lot of work, which seemed to suit him at that stage of his life.

William kept writing and investing in London's Globe Theater and, in 1602, buying a large estate in Old Stratford, north of Stratford-on-Avon, with 127 acres. He was well connected at the courts of the Realm, and when Queen Elizabeth died in 1603, he stayed in favor with her successor, King James I. In June of 1607 his eldest daughter, Susanna, married Dr. John Hall, who was known for his diagnostic skill and herbal practice. This must have given William the opportunity to hone his knowledge of plant lore, herbal remedies, and the symbols associated with plants.

The garden at New Place was redesigned shortly after World War I and incorporates the foundation of the original building. A sunken Elizabethan knot garden sits in the center of the site and is divided into quadrants with a central fountain. An elevated pathway circumnavigates the square garden, part of it running through an apple tunnel allowing for views over the garden on three of its sides. The beds are divided with santolina, box, and rosemary in a scroll pattern with plantings of many different annuals. Each quadrant has a rose in standard form anchoring the center of the bed. The belfry of the Guild Chapel is visible from the garden, behind which stand the Guildhall and grammar school William attended.

The Great Garden sits behind the Elizabethan Garden and has a long herbaceous border framed by extraordinary box and yew hedges that have taken on a character all their own. Next to the house of Thomas Nash, who married Shakespeare's granddaughter, an herb garden grows among the old foundations where New Place stood.

William Shakespeare died at New Place in the spring of 1616, and was buried in Holy Trinity Church, Stratford, where he had been baptized in April of 1564.

Opposite: Box and yew hedges in the Great Garden at New Place.
Overleaf: The Knot Garden at New Place.

Hatfield House, HERTFORDSHIRE

THE GARDENS OF HATFIELD HOUSE WERE BEGUN BETWEEN 1607 AND 1612 FOR ROBERT CECIL, the first Earl of Salisbury. This work was underway during the latter part of Shakespeare's life, and though there is no evidence that Shakespeare visited Hatfield House, he would have been familiar with the plants and herbals employed by Cecil's gardener and plant collector, the great John Tradescant the Elder. This would include such herbals as *De historia stirpium* by Leonard Fuchs (1542) and William Turner's *New Herbal* (1551). One of the famous botanists of the period, John Gerard, worked with Robert Cecil's father, Lord Burghley, on his garden at Theobalds. *Gerard's Herbal* would have been familiar to Shakespeare as well.

Books about plants were much sought after, new plants and their discovery being an ongoing fascination for the rich and cultured. A hunger for the new and unusual was born with the Renaissance, and although slow to arrive in England, acquired a rich tradition in horticulture and literature. So the gardens of Hatfield were designed and planted with the best knowledge of the time and were of considerable importance.

John Tradescant was sent to the Continent in 1611 to acquire both the best of the ordinary and of the new and unusual for the garden; this included different roses, tulips, anemones, fritillaries, martagon lilies, and, most important, fruit trees: cherry, apple, pear, mulberry, apricot, peach, and medlar. The term "outlandish" was coined for plants not native to England, and many were tried that could not weather the English climate. Most Tudor gardens laid out at that time were later replaced in the eighteenth-century landscape movement or underwent various stages of renovation.

Opposite: The Palace Knot Garden with the Old Palace behind it.
Above: A niche in the Old Riding School.

In 1972, the present Dowager Marchioness of Salisbury rekindled an interest in the Hatfield House gardens, re-creating them in the "feel and manner of a Jacobean garden" to suit the house, which had changed little since its building. Employing the extensive garden library resources still at Hatfield House as well as other sources, Lady Salisbury created marvelous Jacobean-style gardens. Similar work was undertaken at the country residence at Cranborne, in Dorset, where John Tradescant had also been involved in the planting. Great care was taken in the plant material and design of the gardens, and now they also beautifully evoke that period.

The gardens were not created as Shakespearean gardens, but are a true representation of a stately home garden of his time. Hatfield House has extensive parklands and many gardens, but the three most relevant to this book are close by the Old Palace. This building dates from between 1480 and 1497 as the Palace of the Bishops of Ely, but it was taken up by Henry the VIII in 1538 to be used as a nursery for his children, Mary, Edward, and Elizabeth. When Queen Elizabeth ascended the throne in 1558, she held her first Council of State in the Great Hall of the Old Palace. It is in front of this historic building that the Palace Knot Garden is placed. A sunken garden, it is designed to be viewed from above by walking around its surrounding grassed embankment. The sloping edges are sown with wildflowers and the garden itself is surrounded with a hawthorn hedge accented with topiary in arch and umbrella forms. The knots are created with box and planted with a wide variety of plants from the period, creating a mix of blooming colors. Two honeysuckle arbors anchor a lateral axis with a central fountain and a gilded statue. One section of the garden is laid out as a boxwood maze up to about eighteen inches high with gravel between. It was customary in that period for a maze to be low in height and part of a knot garden.

The West Parterre Garden sits beside the portion of Hatfield House that Robert Cecil built and is enclosed with a pleached lime walk. The garden's central fountain may be a surviving element of the French engineer Salomon de Caux's work, around which flower beds fan out, cutting into grass pathways surrounded by a yew hedge. To one side stands a mulberry tree planted by James I. The garden has an extensive collection of dianthus and colorful blooms: poppies, peonies, roses, lilies, iris, and alliums abound. The surrounding yew hedge's sides are slightly curved, and each corner bulges out with a tall circular turret of yew accented with a ball on each side.

The scented garden features a central sundial surrounded by honeysuckles pruned to standard form and various herbs—sage, hyssop, sweet cecily, and anise. It is enclosed by a brick wall hung with aromatic vines.

Boxwood is used extensively throughout the gardens, creating arches, balls, and every manner of form. Some is used to separate rooms or alleys or to encompass a fountain. This creates a wealth of green as the backbone of the gardens, set against the old red bricks. The gardens of Hatfield are of another era, and a tribute to all who have worked on them.

Opposite: Wildflower bank surrounding the Palace Knot Garden.
Overleaf left: Standard honeysuckle in the Scented Garden.
Overleaf right: Alliums in front of a yew-hedge corner of the West Parterre Garden.

Cranborne Manor, DORSET

CRANBORNE, A HUNTING ESTATE DATING BACK TO THE TWELFTH CENTURY, WAS GRANTED TO Robert Cecil at about the same time that he received Hatfield House from King James I as a reward for his help in smoothing the transition from the Tudor to the Stuart monarchy. John Tradescant the Elder was employed in some of the design and tree planting.

Sir Francis Bacon might have been describing a mount garden at Cranborne in his "Essay of Gardens" when he wrote: "At the end of both the side grounds I would have a mount of some pretty height, leaving the wall of the enclosure breast high, to look abroad into the fields. . . . Little low hedges, round like welts, with some pretty pyramids, I like well, and in some places fair columns upon frames of carpenter's work." The White Garden also fits the description for fruit trees, which he suggested should be planted in beds: "And this would be generally observed, that the borders wherein you plant your fruit-trees be fair and large and low (and not steep) and set with fine flowers, but thin and sparingly lest they deceive the trees." Bacon's thoughts on the "style of good gardening" were both opinionated and practical, leaving us good directions for re-creating gardens evocative of that period.

Cranborne's gardens are mostly enclosed spaces, each with its own identity and purpose, with magnificent avenues of beech, lime, and yew creating axes through the property. Every now and again a view is afforded through gates or openings in the hedges that show the surrounding fields. The feeling of house and gardens being solidly grounded in the country and of the seasons' passing in an orderly manner infuse the place. One can easily imagine Shakespeare writing *The Merry Wives of Windsor* or *A Midsummer Night's Dream* there had he been able to sit in these gardens.

Opposite: The mound in the Sundial Garden.
Above: The Green Garden.

Above left: Summer flowering border edges the Church Walk.
Right: Apple trees in the White Garden.

Above: The Bowling Alley.
Opposite: Herbaceous borders and curving yew hedges in the Chalk Walk Garden.

Opposite: Entrance to the Herb Garden.

Above: Main vista out of the White Garden into the surrounding countryside.

MUSEUM OF GARDEN HISTORY

St. Mary-at-Lambeth, LONDON

STANDING ALONGSIDE LAMBETH PALACE, THE CENTER OF THE ANGLICAN COMMUNITY, ON THE South Bank of the Thames is a small church called St. Mary-at-Lambeth. The church was deconsecrated in 1972 and set for demolition in 1976. When John and Rosemary Nicholson realized that the graves of the two plant collectors John Tradescant the Elder and Younger rested there, they determined to save the building. Understanding the significance of the Tradescants to gardening in England, in 1977 they created a trust for the Museum of Garden History. The church building was thereby saved, and the Museum was formally opened by the Queen Mother in 1983.

The Dowager Marchioness of Salisbury helped to design and plant an appropriate knot garden for the small courtyard with plant material from the seventeenth century. Knot gardens became fashionable in the middle of the fifteenth century in England and reflected the action of tying something together that was so much a part of that era. Early knot gardens mostly used woody herbs for their hedges, until John Parkinson's 1639 *Paradisi in sole paradisus terrestris, or A Garden of All Sorts of Pleasant Flowers which Our English Ayre Will Permit* advanced the use of box. The knot garden at St. Mary's is planted with dwarf box in an intricate design: a square, a circle within that, with four half-circles touching in the center, and with an inner, smaller square with arms to the larger square. Knots can be of whatever design one is able to create, but care must be taken to allow the plants room to grow between the hedges that form framing compartments. Knot gardens became very popular in Tudor times as a means of highlighting new plants as they were introduced to England.

Opposite: The center of the knot garden is anchored by a holly topiary.
Above: Garden ornaments in the square knot garden.

A topiary of the variegated holly 'Golden King' in the middle gives the garden a central structure. Myrtle, viburnum, rosemary, teucrium, and sea buckthorn are also topiaried to form other sculptural elements. The compartments are planted with a variety of shrubs, perennials, and bulbs. There are several different species of roses, while a large bush of *rosa x alba 'maxima'* climbs one of the church walls. The knot design creates four separate T's—for the Tradescants—and these are planted either in *Santolina chamaecyparissus* or *Helichrysum italicum,* as opposed to the dwarf box for the rest of the hedges, thus adding a different color and emphasis.

The garden is located not far from where the Tradescants had their own museum of novelties and oddities, The Ark. They traveled far and wide, returning with new curios both "natural and unnatural" for the collection, which was one of the first of its kind. The Ark was visited by the rich and also by local Londoners who were prepared to pay to view the oddities. Elias Ashmole became friends with the Tradescants and, through questionable means, obtained the collection on John the Younger's death and gave it to Oxford University in his own name.

The garden is a fine tribute to the relationship between the Salisbury family and the Tradescants and their combined contribution to gardening—from Shakespeare's time to the present.

Above left: A white climbing rose at the church entrance.
Above right: A stone bench nestled in shrubbery.
Opposite: The knot garden in front of the tomb of Admiral Bligh, who captained the H.M.S. Bounty.

Shakespeare Garden, Central Park

NEW YORK CITY

SHAKESPEARE HAS BEEN STANDING PROUD IN CENTRAL PARK SINCE 1872, IN THE FORM OF A statue by John Quincy Adams Ward near the start of the Literary Walk. A Shakespeare garden was started in 1916, replacing a Victorian "Garden of the Heart" on a site to the west of Belvedere Castle. The site is very steep and a large part is rock outcropping. The fledgling Shakespeare Garden went through half a century of neglect and revival, and by the 1960s very little was left except a mulberry tree thought to have been grown from a slip taken from a mulberry tree at Shakespeare's Birth Place, in Stratford-on-Avon.

In 1980, a turning point occurred for Central Park with the formation of the Central Park Conservancy, a foundation that raised funds through private sources to help the Parks Department of the City of New York. The Conservancy recognized the importance of Central Park to New York City and started fundraising and restoration of the park on a formidable scale. In 1986, the Samuel and May Rudin Foundation gave funds to restore the Shakespeare Garden under the auspices of the Conservancy; the landscape designers Bruce Kelly and David Varnell were consulted, and a new era began.

The concept for the garden was that it be wild and romantic, which was more attuned to the steep nature of the site than a formal design unsuited to the gradient. The straight pathways were rerouted to curve around the steep hill and were lined with Adirondack-style rustic cedar fences and benches. The plantings were chosen for their durability in the difficult New York City environment and are as close to Shakespearean flowers as can flourish in the local climate. Drifts of flowers were planted to create swaths of color and form, moving with the contours of the hill. Splashes of poppies, delphinium, and geranium intermingle with

Opposite: Curving pathways and cedar fencing.
Above: Ferns.
Overleaf: Swaths of color in the plantings.

various forms of grasses. Red and blue drifts of tulips underplanted with grape hyacinth form a dramatic palette in the spring. Several

kinds of roses were planted along the fences that cascade down the rock faces, including Lancaster, York, musk, and Gallica varieties.

Large banks of ferns are highlighted with narcissus and purple allium.

Above: *Rosa rugosa* spills over cedar fencing.
Opposite: Tulips and blue hyacinth.

The Shakespeare Garden, Vassar College

POUGHKEEPSIE, NEW YORK

TO COMMEMORATE THE THREE-HUNDREDTH YEAR SINCE SHAKESPEARE'S DEATH, VASSAR COLLEGE'S English and botany departments collaborated to create a Shakespeare garden. Vassar College had distinctively English roots; its founder, Matthew Vassar, was born in Norfolk, England, and emigrated with his father to America in 1796. He had a brewery business in Poughkeepsie, New York, before founding the college in 1861. In 1916, when the garden was initiated, the college president was Dr. Henry Noble MacCracken, a noted Chaucer scholar who no doubt encouraged the endeavor.

The Shakespeare Garden sits on a south-facing slope at the bottom of which flows the Fonteyn Kill River, its bank lined with tall weeping willows that veil the view of neighboring college buildings. Two pathways, bordered by raised flower beds, form the main axis. The formality of the design mimics the Elizabethan style, and side hedges of hemlock lend a feeling of enclosure. Where the two pathways intersect, a sundial forms a visual anchor. The lower transverse pathway is capped at either end with arched walkways.

Initially, seeds for the garden were obtained from Stratford-on-Avon, adapting as many plants included in Shakespeare's writings as were viable in the Hudson Valley. All the construction and earth movement was carried out by the women students of that time. The top beds were planted with old roses that overlook the garden; below these the beds were more structured, gridlike plantings of the culinary and medicinal herbs that Shakespeare mentioned. The beds below were set out as knot gardens but have since become flower beds. Boxwood shrubs in ball-like form accent each terrace and give the garden a central backbone.

Some early statuary figures that Matthew Vassar brought back from Italy adorn one of the flower beds, planted with scarlet sage in a theatrical way. Over the last fifteen years, the garden has been adapted to provide students with a place for reflective study.

Opposite: Looking down the garden, over a bed of red sage, toward the weeping willows.
Above: A quiet corner, a feast for the eyes.

Consequently, the plants of the lower beds are now chosen as much to provide interest throughout the year as to correspond with those of which Shakespeare wrote: wisteria, foxgloves, poppies, lilies, sweet William, alliums, pinks, and violas. There is a whimsical feeling to the garden—volunteer plants are encouraged and the river running close beside lends a quiet, bucolic atmosphere.

Opposite: A view across the bottom of the garden, with a sundial and the lower beds.
Above: Individual beds with plant names and Shakespeare quotations.
Overleaf: The lower garden flower beds, with foxgloves and delphiniums.
Second overleaf: Italian statues amid red sage look down upon the garden.

The Shakespeare Garden at the Mayflower Inn

WASHINGTON, CONNECTICUT

THE SHAKESPEARE GARDEN AT THE MAYFLOWER INN IS EXCELLENT BY ANY STANDARD. IT SITS on a gentle slope below the south terrace of the Inn, completely surrounded by a symphony of trees. The main axis of its strong design is a gray stone pathway running the full length of the garden and terminating in a perfectly conical fern-leafed beech tree. The garden is located according to Elizabethan parameters, ideal for viewing from the Inn's terrace above but far enough away to draw one to explore it more intimately. The footprint of the design is the same as that of the Globe Theatre in London—intersecting axes create a large cross when seen in plan.

On entering the garden there is an antechamber with mirrored plantings, running parallel to the pathway, that create strong bands of color and draw one into the garden's main chamber. The tulips and Johnny jump-ups that are used in the spring are switched to blue petunias and purple sage in summer, backed by groupings of roses and perennials. The main chamber is a knot garden divided into quadrants, with box enclosing three beds in each quarter and one free-floating unenclosed bed. A meandering pathway created by pavers placed in the center of the garden circumnavigates these beds and is anchored with a bronze bust of Shakespeare sculpted by H. Muller. A transverse axis is anchored at each end by arched arbors of wisteria and mandevilla accompanied by stone benches, creating a quiet place to retreat and mull over some of the Shakespearean quotations that are set on bronze plaques around the garden.

Each of the quadrants' corner beds has a cherry tree underplanted with bulbs in spring and daisies in summer. Two sets of urns provide further structure by anchoring each corner and enclosing the statue of the Bard. The knot beds are planted with tulips and daffodils in early spring and are later filled with lady's mantle, catmint, iris, daisies, snapdragons, foxgloves, nicotiana, phlox, astilbes,

Opposite: Early spring, with tulips, looking down the axis of the garden.
Above: Central to the garden is a bust of the Bard.

Above: Lilies in a flower bed.
Right: Summer, looking up a curving pathway through the garden.

silver dust, cosmos, lilies, and sedums, all intermingled to give a variety of color. The free-form beds are planted with large swaths of blue sage in summer. Butterflies flit around the large buddleia bushes that flank either side of the arched arbors.

The fine choice of Shakespeare texts on the plaques is in keeping with the strong design and comes from the ardent love of Shakespeare held by the Inn's owners and garden creators, Adriana Mnuchin and her daughter Lisa Adelow Hedley. Adriana, an able businesswoman, is co-founder and chairwoman of the Board of Trustees of the Shakespeare Society; Lisa, a filmmaker and lawyer, founded the Children of Difference Foundation. From these strong roots a wonderful garden was created in 1992.

Above: An archway over a bench with buddleia.
Opposite: Early summer, with lavender, looking down the axis of the garden.

$\mathcal{N}$orthwestern $\mathcal{U}$niversity, EVANSTON, ILLINOIS

AT THE TERCENTENNIAL OF SHAKESPEARE'S DEATH IN 1916, WORLD WAR I WAS UNDERWAY. VARIOUS groups across the United States chose the anniversary as an opportunity to show their empathy with England by creating Shakespeare gardens. This was certainly the case in the prosperous township of Evanston, north of Chicago on the shores of Lake Michigan.

In 1910, the Drama League of America was formed in Chicago to stimulate community building and individual enrichment through drama. In 1915, the DLA asked for suggestions on ways to show their union with English culture. A noted landscape architect and member, Jens Jensen, answered with a design for a Shakespeare garden.

An interesting aspect of this story is that Jensen was famed for his Prairie School landscaping, which utilized naturalistic elements and indigenous plantings, and was at the opposite end of the spectrum from formal Elizabethan knot gardens. At the time, he was superintendent of Chicago's West Park System, but he was also an ardent theater lover and was keenly interested in the drama within nature.

Planting was initiated in 1916 and completed in 1920. A double hedge of hawthorn grown from French seedlings created the enclosure of the 120-by-70-foot oblong garden. In 1929, both ends of the garden were anchored by strong elements, an oval bench at the west and a fountain and bust of Shakespeare at the east. The fountain was designed by architect Hubert Burnham and the bronze plaque by sculptor Leon Hermont. A grassed main axis runs the length of the garden and eight beds lie parallel to it. Since 1990, some changes have been implemented at the suggestion of English landscape gardener John Brookes. A sundial placed in the

Opposite: The long central vista from the bottom of the garden toward the fountain.
Above: A pathway with a bench between double hawthorn hedges.
Overleaf: The view down a side path toward a curved bench and a sundial.

garden's center creates a focal point, and the beds along the main axis are now edged with antique bricks instead of being enclosed with box, as the outer ones remain.

The strong double hawthorn hedge and two large hawthorns at each end create the backbone of the design and are one of the reasons why the garden was placed on the National Register of Historic places in 1989. The garden's center has four boxwood rounds that accompany a transverse axis terminating in wooden benches through arched openings in the inner hawthorn hedge. Over the years, the plantings in the beds have developed based on what can survive the extremes of the Evanston climate. The plantings include white, pink, and red roses, lilies, clematis, delphinium, lavender, nasturtiums, parsley, lady's mantle, giant alliums, geraniums, daisies, and various hostas.

Situated as it is within the Northwestern University campus, the garden has buildings close around it, but it is a tranquil place much visited by students and members of the community.

Opposite: The view through an arch, with the University spire behind.
Above: Lush plantings provide color and fragrance.

The Shakespeare Garden, MONTGOMERY, ALABAMA

WHEN THE ALABAMA SHAKESPEARE FESTIVAL IN ANNISTON, ALABAMA, NEARLY CLOSED IN THE 1980s, Carolyn Blount, a board member, asked her husband, Wynton, to help. His response was more than anyone could have dreamed. He proposed a 250-acre cultural park featuring a double theater. The only catch was that it would have to be located in Montgomery. The Blount donation to execute this dream was the single largest donation in the history of American theater, and it put Alabama squarely on the map for magnificent Shakespearean performances.

The large brick theater complex is surrounded by grounds and lakes designed by Russell Page. Not far from the theater, space was allotted for a Shakespeare garden that Edwina Von Gal of New York was commissioned to design. A thatched amphitheater is centrally located in the garden, with seats formed in a gently terraced lawn in front of the stage, the backdrop of the garden behind. Bobby McAlpine designed the thatched theater along with an entrance facility, both of which are reminiscent of Elizabethan structures and establish the tone for the garden.

Four large rectangular beds are divided with willow wattle into diamond shapes with group plantings of pansies, cabbages, leeks, thyme, asiatic lilies, chives, sedges, moneywort, rosemary, and lavender forming large strokes of color. Dwarf yaupon hollies, pruned conically, accent the centers of the beds. Bowers of willows cut and woven together shade benches and have honeysuckle and Lamarque roses climbing through them. In the heat of Alabama, shade is essential. Athena elms, eastern red cedars, sweet gums, and Chinese flame trees create a canopy. In spring, thousands of narcissus bulbs flower throughout the beds and around the sides of the garden.

Opposite: A view from the grass terraces to the thatched theater, with the garden behind.
Above: Entrance to the amphitheater.
Overleaf left: Pansies and hooped wattle fencing.
Overleaf right: A central pot with iris leaves around and an arbor in the distance.

The Gardens of the Stratford Festival

STRATFORD, ONTARIO

IN THE 1830S, SHORTLY AFTER A PORTRAIT OF WILLIAM SHAKESPEARE WAS GIVEN TO THE OWNER of the Shakespeare Hotel, the settlement of Little Thames in Canada changed its name to Stratford. The creek nearby was renamed the Avon River, and when the railroad came through town in the 1850s, Stratford became a provincial center. In 1870, the town bought the Old Grove farm, turned it into parkland, and started acquiring and maintaining parks and gardens.

In 1910, and again in 1922, fires burned the Dufton Woolen Mill, leaving only a 65-foot brick tower standing amid the charred rubble. This eyesore near the center of town was tackled by some visionary citizens, led by Thomas Orr, who persuaded the city to purchase the site in 1925. The chimney was put to use as a purple martin birdhouse, but it proved so popular with the martins that their droppings soon blanketed the garden and the chimney birdhouse had to be closed. Orr researched Shakespearean plants that would be appropriate for the Ontario climate and drew up a list of sixty varieties. Toronto landscape architect H. B. Dunnington Grubb designed the garden, which was officially opened in 1936.

Today, the garden lies alongside the Avon River, with an entrance through a covered gateway accompanied by two weeping mulberry trees. A terraced garden has quartered knot beds enclosed with box placed around a central sundial that was donated by the Rotary Club of Stratford, England. The planting in the knot beds is by pairs, with colored gravel in between. There are two beds of solid orange petunias and two diminutive knot beds made up of santolina and alternanthera.

This terrace overlooks a long herb garden split into four long beds surrounding a central circular bed of lavender from Stratford, England. These beds are partly enclosed by a row of yew columns, along which runs a path with a deep perennial border on the other

Opposite: Looking down on parterres, with the birdhouse tower in the distance.
Above: The covered gateway.

Above: Herbs in a double border.
Right: The New Meighen Garden of perennials, with grass and rivers of thyme.

side. This flower bed is in the process of being replanted with Shakespearean plants. A rose garden, originally holding red and white York and Lancaster roses, is now planted with a single variety, a Tropicana cultivar. A bronze bust of Shakespeare by Cleve Home was added to the rose garden in 1949. Several Shakespearean trees, including cherries, walnuts, crab apples, and oaks, form a parklike area. Wonderful weeping willows line the banks of the Avon.

The herb garden is very full and particularly aromatic when it rains. This was very important to the Elizabethan aesthetic, much more so than it is today. Of course, the medicinal qualities of plants were also more significant then, and the herbalists of the day knew remedies for numerous ailments. The herbs grown here include peppermint, tarragon, lemon balm, dill, horehound, garlic chives, chives, top onion, costmary, salad burnet, sage, pineapple sage, wild marjoram, summer savory, winter savory, sweet basil, catnip, horseradish, rosemary, lavender, French sorrel, angelica, lady's mantle, coriander, bergamot, spearmint, lovage, yellow bedstraw, chervil, garlic, rue, thyme and fennel.

The parks and gardens of Stratford developed into a park system running along the river that was unique for its time and brought the city much acclaim. Together with that growth came the cultural growth of the town. In 1953, the world-famous Stratford Shakespeare Festival began, originally housed in a large tent landscaped with Lombardy poplars. A permanent modernist building was designed by Robert Fairfield for the Festival in 1957, with contemporary landscaping undertaken by Macklin Hancock.

The gardens were named and funds donated by the family of Arthur Meighen, a former Prime Minister of Canada. They have gone through three phases: the original plantings around the tent; a carpet bedding garden created under the able direction of Dennis Washburn; and, starting in 1996, a perennial garden under the direction of Neil Turnbull using some 250 species of plants from the heirloom varieties. This last was laid out on one side of the building and a formal Elizabethan knot garden was laid out on another.

The perennial garden was designed to have the feeling of a wild garden. Although it is planted in beds surrounded by a grid of slowly descending cement pathways, these are softened by the way the plantings flow one into another. There are three separate thyme beds that flow low, like streams, down the gently sloping hill among the taller plants. The garden is topped by a rectangular pool with water lilies and a fountain. The planting becomes a large carpet, with the different blooms forming swaths of color. The garden is enclosed by a horseshoe road that brings visitors right to the theater doors, and is anchored at the bottom end by a single gingko tree that has two large trunks fanning out its branches into a broad canopy. Large cylindrical concrete columns enclose each side, the modern equivalent of the yew columns. Low wooden benches aligned with the transverse paths blend into the beds and allow people to sit surrounded by the plants. It is, however, mostly seen by people before a theater performance, and there is a sense of excitement as they move through the garden toward their entertainment, noting unusual plants or combinations as they go.

The Elizabethan garden has a very different character, being square, as Sir Francis Bacon suggested, then divided into quadrants, each with a central circular element. Three of these centerpieces are flower beds and the fourth is a large, symbolic sundial with a tin statue of the Bard as the finial. Central to the whole garden is a twelve-sided fountain of black granite inscribed with a quotation from *Cymbeline*: "These flow'rs are like the pleasures of the world." The flower beds are hedged with meticulously pruned boxwood, and some fifty perennials and annuals make up the planting list; included for their fragrance are evening-scented stock, sweet rocket, sweet sultan, and four o'clocks. An annual massed in the circular bed opposite the sundial is love-lies-bleeding, or long purple, which has long plumes of hanging blooms and looks like the kind of plant Shakespeare wrote of in *Hamlet*, Act 4, Scene 7, Line 169:

> There with fantastic garlands did she come
> Of crow-flowers, nettles, daisies, and long purples,
> That liberal shepherds give a grosser name,
> But our cold maids do dead men's fingers call them.

Above: The New Meighen Garden with the lily pond and white columns behind.
Overleaf: The Elizabethan Garden with a round bed in the foreground and the tin statue of Shakespeare behind.

The Shakespeare Garden at the University College of the Fraser Valley, CHILLIWACK, BRITISH COLUMBIA

THE CITY OF CHILLIWACK ON THE FRASER RIVER BEGAN IN 1857 AS A LANDING PLACE FOR THE steamboats that supplied the gold miners farther upriver. Set on the flat, very fertile river plain between two lines of mountains, it is now an agricultural market town. For the millennium, the University College of the Fraser Valley decided to create a Shakespeare garden, engaging the staff and students from the theater, English, agriculture, and health sciences departments in the project. It was seen not only as a multifaceted teaching opportunity for those departments, but also as a community-building experience within the college and local environs.

Horticultural instructor Nancy Moore challenged her students to create a design for the garden that would reflect the middle-class standards, values, and tastes of the 1600s. The garden, which was divided into three phases of installation, had differing design objectives for each phase. The first focused on Elizabethan plant material that would blend into the already-established campus environs, notably a line of linden trees. They would have to be hardy, low maintenance, and drought tolerant. The second phase concentrated on medicinal plants and a handicap-accessible design. This would be done on a manageable slope of the garden, with raised beds tall enough for someone in a wheelchair to work in. The last phase was to depict a scene from *A Midsummer Night's Dream*, Act 2, Scene 1, Line 249:

Opposite: A view of the first phase, with a bench and arbor.
Above: An archway along a path.

I know a bank where the wild thyme blows,

Where oxlips and the nodding violet grows,

Quite over-canopied with luscious woodbine,

With sweet musk-roses and with eglantine . . .

This division of the work enabled three years of students to work on the various challenges within the master garden plan. Much volunteer work was undertaken by the staff of the different departments and the community at large, as one of the mandates for the installation was that it not be a burden on the ground staff. This community involvement has been one of the most successful aspects of the whole project.

The planting in the first phase included heathers, rosemary, witch hazel, flowering currant, and sedges. The bulbs consisted of crocus, daffodils, and bluebells. Growing over a wooden arbor were clematis and honeysuckle. For the medicinal section thyme, rosemary, and chives were planted in the raised beds. Garlic, lavender, grapes, blueberries, echinacea, strawberries, artemisia, santolina, wintergreen, meadowsweet, a medlar tree, a weeping mulberry, and a great deal of heather were also included. The scene taken from *A Midsummer Night's Dream* used violas, pansies, untrimmed boxwood, silver artemisia, and dogwood trees. The garden, although still young, brings many people together and is a favorite haven for students during their breaks.

Above: Plantings evoke a scene from *A Midsummer Night's Dream*.
Opposite: Handicap-accessible herb planters.

Shakespeare Garden at Stanley Park

VANCOUVER, BRITISH COLUMBIA

STANLEY PARK TAKES UP THE WHOLE OF A PENINSULA TO THE NORTH OF THE CITY OF VANCOUVER. It was inaugurated in 1888 by the Governor General of Canada, Lord Stanley. The most striking aspect to a visitor is the size of the trees, particularly the cedars, hemlocks, and firs, which rise majestically in height and form. It is almost fitting that the Shakespeare Garden in Stanley Park today is really only trees.

In 1916, on the tercentenary of Shakespeare's death, the Vancouver Shakespeare Society was formed, and there are records of an oak being planted by the Shakespeare Tercentenary Committee in April of that year. In 1936, a memorial to Shakespeare including several trees planted for the garden was officially inaugurated. Extensive gardens with Elizabethan flowers, trellises, and fountains were planned, but never seem to have been completed. Now the Shakespeare Garden stands somewhat in the shadow of a colorful display of rose gardens that are set just above it on the hill. Still, the garden has its own quiet charm. Mature western red cypresses stand next to western hemlocks; an old yew tree spreads its branches freely. Black locust, oaks, plume cypress, black walnut, eastern white pine, hazel trees, and an Atlas cedar anchor the center of the grouping. The bottom of the garden is enclosed by ten robust Kwanzan cherry trees.

Many of the trees have plaques containing Shakespearean verse and the tree's Latin botanical name. The plaque attached to the soaring western red cedar has a quotation from *Titus Andronicus*, Act 4, Scene 3, Line 47:

Opposite: A single western hemlock tree.
Above: The portrait relief of Shakespeare.

Marcus, we are but shrubs, no cedars we,

No big-boned men framed of the Cyclop's size,

But metal, Marcus, steel to the very back,

Yet wrung with wrongs more than our backs can bear . . .

The Shakespeare monument has a bas-relief of the Bard and beneath it a quotation from Ben Jonson's "Memorial to Shakespeare,"

in which he compares Shakespeare's writings to those of Greece and Rome. He concludes: "He was not of an age, but for all time."

Appropriate for a garden of no flowers, only old, stately trees.

Above: A view from under the Atlas cedar tree toward the Kwanzan cherries.
Opposite: The Shakespeare plaque.

An Illustrated Alphabet of Plants

corn

A MIDSUMMER NIGHT'S DREAM ACT 2. SCENE 1. LINE 26

Robin describes a jealous fight between Oberon and Titania, King and Queen of the fairies.

But she perforce withholds the lovèd boy,
Crowns him with flowers, and makes him all her joy.
And now they never meet in grove, or green,
By fountain clear, or spangled starlight sheen,
But they do square, that all their elves for fear
Creep into acorn cups, and hide them there.

Apple

THE MERCHANT OF VENICE ACT 1. SCENE 3. LINE 96

Antonio and Bassanio negotiate a loan from Shylock; religious undertones cloud the fiscal process.

ANTONIO Mark you this, Bassanio?
The devil can cite Scripture for his purpose.
An evil soul producing holy witness
Is like a villain with a smiling cheek,
A goodly apple rotten at the heart.
O, What a goodly outside falsehood hath!

Apricot

RICHARD II ACT 3. SCENE 4. LINE 30

Gardener talks to two helpers about the state of the country while the Queen eavesdrops.

Go, bind thee up young dangling apricots
Which, like unruly children, make their sire
Stoop with oppression of their prodigal weight.
Give some supportance to the bending twigs.
(To Second Man) Go thou, and, like an executioner,
Cut off the heads of too fast-growing sprays
That look too lofty in our commonwealth.
All must be even in our government.
You thus employed, I will go root away
The noisome weeds which without profit suck
The soil's fertility from wholesome flowers.

Balm

RICHARD II ACT 1. SCENE 1. LINE 165

Thomas Mowbray, accused of murder, embezzlement, and treason, appeals to clear his name.

I am disgraced, impeached and baffled here,
Pierced to the soul with slander's venomed spear,
The which no balm can cure but his heart blood
Which breathed this poison.

Bay

RICHARD II ACT 2. SCENE 4. LINE 7

*Welsh Captain expresses to Lord Salisbury his troops' fears about
King Richard's probable demise.*

'Tis thought the King is dead. We will not stay.

The bay trees in our country are all withered,

And meteors fright the fixèd stars of heaven.

The pale-faced moon looks bloody on the earth,

And lean-looked prophets whisper fearful change.

Birch

MEASURE FOR MEASURE ACT 1. SCENE 3. LINE 23

*The Duke of Vienna says the laws have been allowed to slip and must
be enforced.*

Now, as fond fathers,

Having bound up the threat'ning twigs of birch

Only to stick it in their children's sight

For terror, not to use, in time the rod

More mocked becomes than feared: so our decrees,

Dead to infliction, to themselves are dead;

And Liberty plucks Justice by the nose,

The baby beats the nurse, and quite athwart

Goes all decorum.

lackberry

1 HENRY IV ACT 2. SCENE 5. LINE 409

Sir John Oldcastle (Falstaff) re-enacts King Henry's mockery of his son, Prince Harry.

>   If then thou be son to me,
> here lies the point. Why, being son to me art thou so
> pointed at? Shall the blessed sun of heaven prove a
> micher, and eat blackberries?—A question not to be
> asked. Shall the son of England prove a thief, and take
> purses?—A question to be asked.

$\mathcal{B}$ox

TWELFTH NIGHT, or WHAT YOU WILL ACT 2. SCENE 5. LINE 14

Maria creates a plot to trick love-lost Malvolio.

> Get ye all three into the box-tree. Malvolio's
> coming down this walk. He has been yonder i' the sun
> practicing behaviour to his own shadow this half-hour:
> Observe him, for the love of mockery, for I know this
> letter will make a contemplative idiot of him.

Broom

THE TEMPEST.   ACT 4. SCENE 1. LINE 64

Iris calls on Ceres, Queen of the Sky, to appear from her magical domain.

. . . thy broomgroves,

Whose shadow the dismissèd bachelor loves,

Being lass-lorn . . .

Buttercup

THE TRAGEDY OF KING LEAR ACT 4. SCENE 3. LINE 1

Cordelia looks for her father, King Lear, who has sunk into madness.

Alack, 'tis he! Why, he was met even now,

As mad as the vexed sea, singing aloud,

Crowned with rank fumitor and furrow-weeds,

With burdocks, hemlock, nettles, cuckoo-flowers,

Darnel, and all the idle weeds that grow

In our sustaining corn. A century send forth.

Search every acre in the high-grown field,

And bring him to our eye.

Cabbage

THE MERRY WIVES OF WINDSOR ACT 1. SCENE 1. LINE 108

Sir John Falstaff ridicules his accusers by flippantly accepting his guilt.
(Pauca verba *means "few words remain"*)

SIR JOHN   I will answer it straight: I have done all this.
That is now answered.

SHALLOW   The Council shall know this.

SIR JOHN   'Twere better for you if it were known in counsel.
You'll be laughed at.

SIR HUGH EVANS   *Pauca verba*, Sir John; good worts.

SIR JOHN   Good worts? Good cabbage!

Camomile

1 HENRY IV ACT 2. SCENE 5. LINE 401

*Sir John Oldcastle acts King Henry's part in an imaginary
interview with Prince Harry, to prepare the Prince for an interview
with his father.*

Peace, good pint-pot: peace, good tickle-brain.—
Harry, I do not only marvel where thou spendest thy
time, but also how thou art accompanied. For though
The camomile, the more it is trodden on, the faster it
grows, yet youth, the more it is wasted, the sooner it
wears.

Carnation

THE WINTER'S TALE ACT 4. SCENE 4. LINE 79

Perdita, with a touch of garden snobbery, addresses Polixenes on seasonal plants.

<blockquote>

Sir, the year growing ancient,
Not yet on summer's death, nor on the birth
Of trembling winter, the fairest flowers o'th' season
Are our carnations and streaked gillyvors,
Which some call nature's bastards. Of that kind
Our rustic garden's barren, and I care not
To get slips of them.

</blockquote>

Cedar

RICHARD DUKE OF YORK (3 HENRY VI) ACT 5. SCENE 2. LINE 9

Mortally wounded, Warwick is left to die by King Edward IV, and in his last moments laments his demise and what he had worked and fought for.

<blockquote>

. . . I must yield my body to the earth
And by my fall the conquest to my foe.
Thus yields the cedar to the axe's edge,
Whose arms gave shelter to the princely eagle,
Under whose shade the ramping lion slept,
Whose top-branch overpeered Jove's spreading tree
And kept low shrubs from winter's powerful wind.

</blockquote>

Cherry

ALL IS TRUE (HENRY VIII) ACT 5. SCENE 1. LINE 164

*Old Lady tells King Henry that Queen Katherine has just delivered a
girl, not the boy he so desperately wanted.*

Ay, ay, my liege,
And of a lovely boy. The God of heaven

Both now and ever bless her! 'Tis a girl
Promises boys hereafter. Sir, your queen
Desires your visitation, and to be
Acquainted with this stranger. 'Tis as like you
As cherry is to cherry.

Chestnut

AS YOU LIKE IT ACT 3. SCENE 4. LINE 6

Rosalind and Celia discuss the attributes of Orlando, who has captured Rosalind's heart.

ROSALIND His very hair is of the dissembling colour.

CELIA Something browner than Judas's. Marry, his kisses are Judas's own children.

ROSALIND I'faith, his hair is of a good colour.

CELIA An excellent colour. Your chestnut was ever the only colour.

ROSALIND And his kissing is as full of sanctity as the touch of holy bread.

Columbine

LOVE'S LABOUR'S LOST ACT 5. SCENE 2. LINE 637

Armado, who is imitating the braggart Hector, is mocked by Dumaine, Biron, and Longueville.

ARMADO *(as Hector)* The armipotent Mars, of lances the almighty, Gave Hector a gift—

DUMAINE A gilt nutmeg.

BIRON A lemon.

LONGUEVILLE Stuck with cloves.

DUMAINE No, cloven.

ARMADO Peace!

(as Hector)	The armipotent Mars, of lances the almighty,
	Gave Hector a gift, the heir of Ilion,
	A man so breathèd that certain he would fight, yea,
	From morn till night, out of his pavilion.
	I am that flower—
DUMAINE	That mint.
LONGUEVILLE	That colombine.
ARMADO	Sweet Lord Longueville, rein thy tongue.
LONGUEVILLE	I must rather give it the rein, for it runs against Hector.

*C*rab Apple

THE TRAGEDY OF KING LEAR ACT 1. SCENE 5. LINE 15

King Lear dispatches letters to his three daughters while his fool parodies all their relationships.

FOOL	Shalt see thy other daughter will use thee kindly, for though she's as like this as a crab's like an apple, yet I can tell what I can tell.
LEAR	What canst tell, boy?
FOOL	She will taste as like this as a crab does to a crab.

rown Imperial

THE WINTER'S TALE ACT 4. SCENE 4. LINE 116

Perdita speaks to Florizel.

> O Proserpina,
> For the flowers now that, frighted, thou letst fall
> From Dis's wagon!—daffodils,
> That come before the swallow dares, and take
> The winds of March with beauty; violets, dim,
> But sweeter than the lids of Juno's eyes
> Or Cytherea's breath; pale primroses,
> That die unmarried ere they can behold
> Bright Phoebus in his strength—a malady
> Most incident to maids; bold oxlips, and
> The crown imperial; lilies of all kinds,
> The flower-de-luce being one. O, these I lack,
> To make you garlands of, and my sweet friend,
> To strew him o'er and o'er.

Currant

THE WINTER'S TALE ACT 4. SCENE 3. LINE 35

*The rogue Autolycus and his son the Clown, both planning and
scheming over the sheep shearers' celebration dinner, evaluate a
shopping list his sister has drawn up.*

CLOWN   Let me see, what
am I to buy for our sheep-shearing feast? Three pound
of sugar, five pound of currants, rice—what will this
sister of mine do with rice? But my father hath made
her mistress of the feast, and she lays it on. She hath
made me four-and-twenty nosegays for the shearers—
three-man-song-men, all, and very good ones—but
they are most of them means and basses, but one
Puritan amongst them, and he sings psalms to
hornpipes. I must have saffron to colour the warden
pies; mace; dates, none—that's out of my note;
nutmegs, seven; a race or two of ginger—but that I
may beg; four pounds of prunes, and as many of raisins
o'th' sun.

ypress

THE FIRST PART OF THE CONTENTION

(2 HENRY VI) ACT 3. SCENE 2. LINE 323

Suffolk, manipulated by Queen Margaret, curses his enemies.

Ay, every joint should seem to curse and ban.

And, even now, my burdened heart would break

Should I not curse them. Poison be their drink!

Gall, worse than gall, the daintiest that they taste!

Their sweetest shade a grove of cypress trees!

Their chiefest prospect murd'ring basilisks!

Their softest touch as smart as lizards' stings!

Their music frightful as the serpent's hiss,

And boding screech-owls make the consort full!

All the foul terrors in dark seated hell—

Daffodil

THE WINTER'S TALE ACT 4. SCENE 3. LINE 1

Autolycus sings the joys of the beginning of spring.

When daffodils begin to peer,

    With heigh, the doxy over the dale,

Why then comes in the sweet o'the year,

    For the red blood reigns in the winter's pale.

Dock

THE TEMPEST ACT 2. SCENE 1. LINE 150

The survivors, after being shipwrecked, survey the island they are beached on and see it differently. Gonzalo addresses King Alonso with optimism, while Sebastian and Antonio shadow him with skepticism and sarcasm.

GONZALO *(to Alonso)*	It is foul weather in us all, good sir,
	When you are cloudy.
SEBASTIAN *(to Alonso)*	Fowl weather?
ANTONIO	Very foul.
GONZALO *(to Alonso)*	Had I a plantation of this isle, my lord—
ANTONIO *(to Sebastian)*	He'd sow't with nettle-seed.
SEBASTIAN	Or docks, or mallows.
GONZALO	And were the king on't, what would I do?
SEBASTIAN *(to Antonio)*	Scape being drunk, for want of wine.

Elder

TITUS ANDRONICUS ACT 2. SCENE 3. LINE 271

Saturninus reads a letter that describes where the body of his brother lies.

Look for thy reward
Among the nettles at the elder tree
Which overshades the mouth of that same pit
Where we decreed to bury Bassianus.

Fennel

HAMLET ACT 4. SCENE 5. LINE 179

Ophelia, having been jilted by Hamlet, rambles in apparent madness.

There's fennel for you, and columbines. There's
rue for you, and here's some for me. We may call it
herb-grace o'Sundays. O, you must wear your rue
with a difference. There's a daisy. I would give you
some violets, but they withered all when my father
died. They say he made a good end.

Fern

1 HENRY IV ACT 2. SCENE 1. LINE 85

*Gadshill and Chamberlain talk in the dark of night outside the stables
of an inn on the London Road.*

GADSHILL   We
           steal as in a castle, cocksure; we have the recipe of
           fern-seed, we walk invisible.
CHAMBERLAIN Nay, by my faith, I think you are more
           beholden to the night than to fern-seed for your walking
           invisible.

 ## Fig

OTHELLO ACT 1. SCENE 3. LINE 319

Iago expounds on self will, comparing it with gardening.

Virtue? A fig! 'Tis in ourselves that we are thus or
thus. Our bodies are our gardens, to the which our
wills are gardeners; so that if we will plant nettles or
sow lettuce, set hyssop and weed up thyme, supply it
with one gender of herbs or distract it with many,
either to have it sterile with idleness or manured with
industry, why, the power and corrigible authority of
this lies in our wills.

 ## Flower-de-luce (Iris)

1 HENRY VI ACT 1. SCENE 1. LINE 78

*Messenger, addressing a group of noblemen attending Henry V's
funeral, has just delivered the news that a large part of the English
territory in France has been lost, owing to a lack of soldiers and
resources.*

Awake, awake, English nobility!
Let not sloth dim your honours new-begot.
Cropped are the flower-de-luces in your arms;
Of England's coat, one half is cut away.

Garlic

1 HENRY IV ACT 3. SCENE 1. LINE 155

*Hotspur, talking about his father, the Earl of Northumberland, to his
brother in-law, Mortimer.*

O, he is as tedious
As a tired horse, a railing wife,
Worse than a smoky house. I had rather live
With cheese and garlic, in a windmill, far,
Than feed on cates and have him talk to me
In any summer house in Christendom.

Ginger

HENRY V ACT 3. SCENE 7. LINE 19

*The French dukes Orléans and Bourbon admire their horses' qualities
as they await dawn to battle the English.*

ORLÉANS He's of the colour of the nutmeg.

BOURBON And of the heat of the ginger. It is a beast for
Perseus. He is pure air and fire, and the dull elements
of earth and water never appear in him, but only in
patient stillness while his rider mounts him. He is
indeed a horse, and all other jades you may
call beasts.

Gooseberry

2 HENRY IV ACT 1. SCENE 2. LINE 169

*Sir John Falstaff, being questioned by the Lord Chief Justice,
is as nonsensical and circuitous as ever.*

I cannot tell, virtue is of so little regard in these
costermongers' times that true valour is turned
bearherd; pregnancy is made a tapster, and his quick
wit wasted in giving reckonings; all the other gifts
appertinent to man, as the malice of this age shapes
them, are not worth a gooseberry.

Gorse

THE TEMPEST ACT 4. SCENE 1. LINE 175

The spirit Ariel describes how he led three drunks through the mire.

Then I beat my tabor,
At which like unbacked colts they pricked their ears,
Advanced their eyelids, lifted up their noses
As they smelt music. So I charmed their ears
That calf-like they my lowing followed, through
Toothed briars, sharp furzes, prickling gorse, and thorns,
Which entered their frail shins.

$\mathcal{G}$rape

A MIDSUMMER NIGHT'S DREAM ACT 3. SCENE 1. LINE 156

*Titania, Queen of the Fairies, asks her minions to treat Nick Bottom,
whom she loves, graciously.*

Be kind and courteous to this gentleman.
Hop in his walks, and gambol in his eyes.
Feed him with apricots and dewberries,
With purple grapes, green figs, and mulberries;
The honeybags steal from the humble-bees,
And for night tapers crop their waxen thighs
And light them at the fiery glow-worms' eyes
To have my love to bed, and to arise;
And pluck the wings from painted butterflies
To fan the moonbeams from his sleeping eyes.
Nod to him, elves, and do him courtesies.

rass

THE TEMPEST ACT 4. SCENE 1. LINE 76

Ceres, or the spirit Ariel masquerading as the spirit Ceres, asks the spirit Iris why she was summoned.

Hail, many-coloured messenger, that ne'er
Dost disobey the wife of Jupiter;
Who with thy saffron wings upon my flowers
Diffusest honey-drops, refreshing showers,
And with each end of thy blue bow dost crown
My bosky acres and my unshrubbed down,
Rich scarf to my proud earth. Why hath thy queen
Summoned me hither to this short-grassed green?

*H*arebell

CYMBELINE ACT 4. SCENE 2. LINE 219

Arviragus laments over the dead body of Innogen.

With fairest flowers
Whilst summer lasts and I live here, Fidele,
I'll sweeten thy sad grave. Thou shalt not lack
The flower that's like thy face, pale primrose, nor
The azured harebell, like thy veins; no, nor
The leaf of eglantine, whom not to slander
Outsweetened not thy breath. The ruddock would
With charitable bill—O bill sore shaming
Those rich-left heirs that let their fathers lie

Without a monument!—bring thee all this,

Yea, and furred moss besides, when flowers are none,

To winter-gown thy corpse.

ℋawthorn

A MIDSUMMER NIGHT'S DREAM ACT 1. SCENE 1. LINE 181

Helena wishes she were the object of Demetrius' affections rather than Hermia, whose heart is set on Lysander.

Call you me fair? That 'fair' again unsay.

Demetrius loves your fair—O happy fair!

Your eyes are lodestars, and your tongue's sweet air

More tuneable than lark to shepherd's ear

When wheat is green, when hawthorn buds appear.

ℋazel

THE TAMING OF THE SHREW ACT 2. SCENE 1. LINE 247

Petruccio denounces false reports of Katherine's qualities.

Why does the world report that Kate doth limp?

O sland'rous world! Kate like the hazel twig

Is straight and slender, and as brown in hue

As hazelnuts, and sweeter than the kernels.

O let me see thee walk. Thou dost not halt.

Heather

THE TEMPEST ACT 1. SCENE 1. LINE 61

In the middle of a violent storm at sea, the ship is breaking apart and all seems lost. Gonzalo calls out for some dry land.

Now would I give a thousand furlongs of sea
for an acre of barren ground: long heath, broom, furze,
anything. The wills above be done, but I would fain
die a dry death.

Holly

AS YOU LIKE IT ACT 2. SCENE 7. LINE 175

Amiens sings a ballad to entertain Duke Senior and Orlando.

Blow, blow, thou winter wind,
Thou art not so unkind
    As man's ingratitude.
Thy tooth is not so keen,
Because thou art not seen,
    Although thy breath be rude.
Hey-ho, sing hey-ho, unto the green holly.
Most friendship is feigning, most loving, mere folly.
    Then hey-ho, the holly;
    This life is most jolly.

Freeze, freeze, thou bitter sky,
That dost not bite so nigh
    As benefits forgot.
Though thou the waters warp,
Thy sting is not so sharp
    As friend remembered not.
Hey-ho, sing hey-ho, unto the green holly.
Most friendship is feigning, most loving, mere folly.
    Then hey-ho, the holly;
    This life is most jolly.

Honeysuckle

MUCH ADO ABOUT NOTHING ACT 3. SCENE 1. LINE6

Hero suggests to Margaret that she set a trap for Beatrice.

> Say that thou overheard'st us
> And bid her steal into the pleachèd bower
> Where honeysuckles, ripened by the sun,
> Forbid the sun to enter—like favourites
> Made proud by princes, that advance their pride
> Against that power that bred it.

Ivy

THE COMEDY OF ERRORS ACT 2. SCENE 2. LINE 176

Adriana mistakes her husband's twin brother for her husband.

Come, I will fasten on this sleeve of thine.
Thou art an elm, my husband; I a vine,
Whose weakness, married to thy stronger state,
Makes me with thy strength to communicate.
If aught possess thee from me, it is dross,
Usurping ivy, brier, or idle moss,
Who, all for want of pruning, with intrusion
Infect thy sap, and live on thy confusion.

$\mathcal{L}$avender

THE WINTER'S TALE ACT 4. SCENE 4. LINE 97

Polixenes and Perdita on plant worthiness and snobbery (see Carnation).

POLIXENES Then make your garden rich in gillyvors,
          And do not call them bastards.

PERDITA   I'll not put
          The dibble in earth to set one slip of them,
          No more than, were I painted, I would wish

This youth should say 'twere well, and only therefore
Desire to breed by me. Here's flowers for you:
Hot lavender, mints, savory, marjoram,
The marigold, that goes to bed wi'th' sun,
And with him rises, weeping. These are flowers
Of middle summer, and I think they are given
To men of middle age. You're very welcome.
She gives him flowers

eek

HENRY V ACT 5. SCENE 1. LINE 23

The Welsh Captain Fluellen forces Ensign Pistol to eat some leek, the Welsh national plant, after Pistol derides it.

PISTOL   Hence! I am qualmish at the smell of leek.

FLUELLEN I peseech you heartily, scurvy lousy knave, at
my desires and my requests and my petitions, to eat,
look you, this leek. Because, look you, you do not love
it, nor your affections and your appetites and your
digestions does not agree with it, I would desire you
to eat it.

ily

CYMBELINE ACT 4. SCENE 2. LINE 202

Guiderius addresses the body of Innogen as it is carried by his brother Arviragus from a cave.

O sweetest, fairest lily!
My brother wears thee not one half so well
As when thou grew'st thyself.

Marigold

PERICLES, PRINCE OF TYRE SCENE 15. LINE 65

*Marina, daughter of Pericles, muses innocently about her life while
left vulnerable to the schemes of Dionyza, the murderer who has
bribed Leonine to kill her. (Tellus means earth)*

No, I will rob Tellus of her weed
To strew thy green with flow'rs: the yellows, blues,

The purple violets and marigolds,
Shall as a carpet hang upon thy tomb,
While summer days doth last. Ay me, poor maid,
Born in a tempest, when my mother died,
This world to me is but a ceaseless storm
Whirring me from my friends.

Marjoram

ALL'S WELL THAT ENDS WELL ACT 4. SCENE 5. LINE 13

The old Lord Lafeu is mimicked by the clown Lavatch as he laments the supposed death of Helen.

LAFEU 'Twas a good lady, 'twas a good lady. We may
pick a thousand salads ere we light on such another
herb.

LAVATCH Indeed, sir, she was the sweet marjoram of the
salad, or rather the herb of grace.

LAFEU They are not grass, you knave, they are nose-herbs.

Medlar

TIMON OF ATHENS ACT 4. SCENE 3. LINE 302

Apemantus spars with Timon.

APEMANTUS The middle of humanity thou never knewest,
but the extremity of both ends. When thou wast in thy
gilt and in thy perfume, they mocked thee for too much
curiosity; in thy rags thou know'st none, but art
despised for the contrary. There's a medlar for thee;
eat it.

TIMON On what I hate I feed not.

APEMANTUS Dost hate a medlar?

TIMON Ay, though it look like thee.

APEMANTUS An thou'dst hated meddlers sooner, thou
shouldst have loved thyself better now.

Moss

TITUS ANDRONICUS ACT 2. SCENE 3. LINE 93

*Tamora accuses Lavinia and Bassianus of luring her into a foul place,
and tries to provoke her sons into killing both.*

A barren detested vale you see it is;

The trees, though summer, yet forlorn and lean,

Overcome with moss and baleful mistletoe.

Here never shines the sun, here nothing breeds

Unless the nightly owl or fatal raven,

And when they showed me this abhorrèd pit

They told me here at dead time of the night

A thousand fiends, a thousand hissing snakes,

Ten thousand swelling toads, as many urchins

Would make such fearful and confusèd cries

As any mortal body hearing it

Should straight fall mad or else die suddenly.

No sooner had they told this hellish tale

But straight they told me they would bind me here

Unto the body of a dismal yew

And leave me to this miserable death.

Mulberry

CORIOLANUS ACT 3. SCENE 2. LINE 73

*Volumnia coaches her son Coriolanus on how to quell an angry mob in
the marketplace.*

Go to them with this bonnet in thy hand,

And thus far having stretched it—here be with them—

Thy knee bussing the stones—for in such business

Action is eloquence, and the eyes of th' ignorant

More learnèd than the ears—waving thy head,

With often, thus, correcting thy stout heart,

Now humble as the ripest mulberry

That will not hold the handling . . .

Mushroom

THE TEMPEST ACT 5. SCENE 1. LINE 33

Prospero addresses the various fairies and spirits as he prepares to place a charm on his brothers and friends.

Ye elves of hills, brooks, standing lakes and groves,
And ye that on the sands with printless foot
Do chase the ebbing Neptune, and do fly him
When he comes back; you demi-puppets that
By moonshine do the green sour ringlets make
Whereof the ewe not bites; and you whose pastime
Is to make midnight mushrooms, that rejoice
To hear the solemn curfew . . .

Mustard

THE TAMING OF THE SHREW ACT 4. SCENE 3. LINE 20

Grumio taunts hungry Katherine.

GRUMIO   What say you to a piece of beef, and mustard?

KATHERINE   A dish I do love to feed upon.

GRUMIO   Ay, but the mustard is too hot a little.

KATHERINE   Why then, the beef, and let the mustard rest.

GRUMIO   Nay, then I will not. You shall have the mustard,
Or else you get no beef of Grumio.

KATHERINE   Then both, or one, or anything thou wilt.

GRUMIO   Why then, the mustard without the beef.

Myrtle

MEASURE FOR MEASURE ACT 2. SCENE 2. LINE 117

*Isabella attempts to dissuade Lucio from executing her brother
Claudio for making Juliet pregnant (although they were betrothed, it
was not sanctioned by the church) by outlining the danger of harsh
justice.*

Merciful heaven,
Thou rather with thy sharp and sulphurous bolt
Split'st the unwedgeable and gnarlèd oak
Than the soft myrtle. But man, proud man,
Dressed in a little brief authority,
Most ignorant of what he's most assured,
His glassy essence, like an angry ape
Plays such fantastic tricks before high heaven
As makes the angels weep, who, with our spleens,
Would all themselves laugh mortal.

$\mathcal{O}$ak

CYMBELINE ACT 4. SCENE 2. LINE 265

Arviragus (with Guiderius) prepares the burial of beheaded Cloten.

Fear no more the frown o'th' great,
    Thou art past the tyrant's stroke.
Care no more to clothe and eat,
    To thee the reed is as the oak.
The sceptre, learning, physic, must
All follow this and come to dust.

$\mathcal{N}$arcissus

ANTONY AND CLEOPATRA ACT 2. SCENE 5. LINE 93

Cleopatra castigates a messenger for bringing her the bad news that Antony married Octavia on his return to Rome.

MESSENGER Should I lie, madam?
CLEOPATRA O, I would thou didst,
    So half my Egypt were submerged and made
    A cistern for scaled snakes. Go, get thee hence.
    Hadst thou Narcissus in thy face, to me
    Thou wouldst appear most ugly. He is married?

$\mathcal{O}$live

TIMON OF ATHENS ACT 5. SCENE 5. LINE 87

Alcibiades' closing lines strike a hopeful note of turning to more peaceful times.

        Bring me into your city,
And I will use the olive with my sword,
Make war breed peace, make peace stint war, make each
Prescribe to other as each other's leech.
Let our drums strike.

nion

ANTONY AND CLEOPATRA ACT 1. SCENE 2. LINE 152

Enobarbus counsels Antony not to return to Rome because of his wife Fulvia's recent death.

Why, sir, give the gods a thankful sacrifice.
When it pleaseth their deities to take the wife of a man
from him, it shows to man the tailors of the earth;
comforting therein that when old robes are worn out
there are members to make new. If there were no more
women but Fulvia, then had you indeed a cut, and the
case to be lamented. This grief is crowned with consola-
tion; your old smock brings forth a new petticoat, and
indeed the tears live in an onion that should water this
sorrow.

Orange

MUCH ADO ABOUT NOTHING ACT 4. SCENE 1. LINE 31

Claudio accuses Hero on the eve of their marriage.

There, Leonato, take her back again.
Give not this rotten orange to your friend.
She's but the sign and semblance of her honour.
Behold how like a maid she blushes here!
O, what authority and show of truth
Can cunning sin cover itself withal!
Comes not that blood as modest evidence

To witness simple virtue? Would you not swear,
All you that see her, that she were a maid,
By these exterior shows? But she is none.
She knows the heat of a luxurious bed.
Her blush is guiltiness, not modesty.

ansy

HAMLET ACT 4. SCENE 5. LINE 175

Ophelia in her apparent madness (see Fennel).

There's rosemary, that's for remembrance. Pray,
love, remember. And there is pansies; that's for
thoughts.

Pea

1 HENRY IV ACT 2. SCENE 1. LINE 8

Second Carrier complains about the state of the house, an allegory for the state of the nation.

Peas and beans are as dank here as a
dog, and that is the next way to give poor jades the
bots. This house is turned upside down since Robin
Ostler died.

Peach

MEASURE FOR MEASURE ACT 4. SCENE 3. LINE 1

The clown Pompey goes through a list of characters assembled in the prison, recounting their crimes and noting that most of them had visited the house of the bawd Mistress Overdone, his employer.

I am as well acquainted here as I was in our house of profession. One would think it were Mistress Overdone's own house, for here be many of her old customers. First, here's young Master Rash; he's in for a commodity of brown paper and old ginger, nine score and seventeen pounds, of which he made five marks ready money. Marry, then ginger was not much in request, for the old women were all dead. Then is there here one Master Caper, at the suit of Master Threepile the mercer, for some four suits of peach-coloured satin, which now peaches him a beggar.

Peony

THE TEMPEST ACT 4. SCENE 1. LINE 64

Iris addresses Ceres.

Thy banks with peonied and twillèd brims
Which spongy April at thy hest betrims . . .

ine

2 HENRY VI ACT 2. SCENE 3. LINE 45

Suffolk describes the diminished authority of Gloucester.

Thus droops this lofty pine and hangs his sprays;

Thus Eleanor's pride dies in her youngest days.

lum

VARIOUS POEMS #10, FROM THE PASSIONATE PILGRIM LINE 1

Sweet rose, fair flower, untimely plucked, soon faded—

Plucked in the bud and faded in the spring;

Bright orient pearl, alack, too timely shaded;

Fair creature, killed too soon by death's sharp sting,

    Like a green plum that hangs upon a tree

    And falls through wind before the fall should be.

$\mathcal{P}$omegranate

ALL'S WELL THAT ENDS WELL ACT 2. SCENE 3. LINE 256

Lafeu derides Paroles, a younger man of lower social standing.

Go to, sir. You were beaten in Italy for picking a
kernel out of a pomegranate, you are a vagabond and
no true traveller, you are more saucy with lords and
honourable personages than the commission of your
birth and virtue gives you heraldry. You are not worth
another word, else I'd call you knave. I leave you.

$\mathcal{P}$oppy

OTHELLO ACT 3. SCENE 3. LINE 326

*Iago, Othello's standard bearer, watches his master enter consumed
with thoughts of his wife's possible infidelities, an idea Iago himself
has planted.*

Trifles light as air
Are to the jealous confirmations strong
As proofs of holy writ. This may do something.
The Moor already changes with my poison.
Dangerous conceits are in their natures poisons,
Which at the first are scarce found to distaste,
But, with a little act upon the blood,
Burn like the mines of sulphur.

Potato

Enter Othello

I did say so.

Look where he comes. Not poppy nor mandragora

Nor all the drowsy syrups of the world

Shall ever medicine thee to that sweet sleep

Which thou owedst yesterday.

THE MERRY WIVES OF WINDSOR ACT 5. SCENE 5. LINE 16

Sir John Falstaff, dressed as Herne the hunter with deer antlers, is taking part in pranks in Windsor Wood when he encounters Mistress Ford.

MISTRESS FORD Sir John! Art thou there, my deer, my
male deer?

SIR JOHN My doe with the black scut! Let the sky rain
potatoes, let it thunder to the tune of 'Greensleeves',
hail kissing-comfits, and snow eringoes; let there come
a tempest of provocation, I will shelter me here.

rimrose

A MIDSUMMER'S NIGHT DREAM ACT 1. SCENE 1 LINE 214

Hermia, who is duty bound to marry Demetrius, has her heart set on Lysander and plans to elope with him to Athens. She shares her plans with Helena.

And in the wood where often you and I
Upon faint primrose beds were wont to lie,
Emptying our bosoms of their counsel sweet,
There my Lysander and myself shall meet . . .

Rhubarb

MACBETH   ACT 5. SCENE 3. LINE 57

Macbeth, his dark mood growing desperate, calls to the doctor to purge his wife of her madness and rid him of the English.

MACBETH   What rhubarb, cyme, or what
purgative drug
Would scour these English hence? Hear'st thou
of them?

DOCTOR   Ay, my good lord. Your royal preparation
Makes us hear something.

MACBETH   *(to an attendant)*   Bring it after me.
I will not be afraid of death and bane
Till Birnam Forest come to Dunsinane.

ose

ROMEO AND JULIET ACT 2. SCENE 1. LINE 84

Juliet speaks to Romeo on discovering he is from a rival family.

O, be some other name!
What's in a name? That which we call a rose
By any other word would smell as sweet.

osemary

ROMEO AND JULIET ACT 4. SCENE 4. LINE 104

Friar Laurence tries to console Capulet for Juliet's death.

She's not well married that lives married long,
But she's best married that dies married young.
Dry up thy tears, and stick your rosemary
On this fair corpse, and, as the custom is,
All in her best array bear her to church;
For though fond nature bids us all lament,
Yet nature's tears are reason's merriment.

Rush

THE TWO NOBLE KINSMEN ACT 4. SCENE 1. LINE 82

The Wooer of the Jailer's daughter recounts to the Jailer how he saw her by the lake.

WOOER   The place

Was knee-deep where she sat; her careless tresses
A wreath of bull-rush rounded; about her stuck
Thousand freshwater flowers of several colours—
That she appeared, methought, like the fair nymph
That feeds the lake with waters, or as Iris
Newly dropped down from heaven. Rings she made
Of rushes that grew by, and to 'em spoke
The prettiest posies—'Thus our true love's tied',
'This you may lose, not me', and many a one.
And then she wept, and sung again, and sighed—
And with the same breath smiled and kissed her
                hand.

Rue

RICHARD II ACT 3. SCENE 4. LINE 103

Gardener replies to the Queen, who had cursed his grafted plants when she learned of the predicted demise of Richard II.

Poor Queen, so that thy state might be no worse
I would my skill were subject to thy curse.
Here did she fall a tear. Here in this place
I'll set a bank of rue, sour herb-of-grace.
Rue even for ruth here shortly shall be seen
In the remembrance of a weeping queen.

trawberry

HENRY V ACT 1. SCENE 1. LINE 61

*Ely refers to young King Henry's surprising abilities despite his
wayward youth.*

The strawberry grows underneath the nettle,
And wholesome berries thrive and ripen best
Neighboured by fruit of baser quality;
And so the Prince obscured his contemplation
Under the veil of wildness—which, no doubt,
Grew like the summer grass, fastest at night,
Unseen, yet crescive in his faculty.

histle

A MIDSUMMER NIGHT'S DREAM ACT 4. SCENE 1. LINE 10

*Nick Bottom, the weaver, tells the fairy Cobweb to get him a
honeybag.*

Monsieur Cobweb, good monsieur, get you your
weapons in your hand and kill me a red-hipped humble-
bee on the top of a thistle; and, good monsieur, bring
me the honeybag. Do not fret yourself too much in the
action, monsieur; and, good monsieur, have a care the
honeybag break not. I would be loath to have you
overflowen with a honeybag, signor.

hyme

A MIDSUMMER NIGHT'S DREAM ACT 2. SCENE 1. LINE 249

Oberon tells Robin Goodfellow to drug Titania in her sleep.

I know a bank where the wild thyme blows,

Where oxlips and the nodding violet grows,

Quite overcanopied with luscious woodbine,

With sweet musk-roses, and with eglantine.

There sleeps Titania sometime of the night,

Lulled in these flowers with dances and delight;

And there the snake throws her enamelled skin,

Weed wide enough to wrap a fairy in;

And with the juice of this I'll streak her eyes,

And make her full of hateful fantasies.

ine

HENRY V ACT 5. SCENE 2. LINE 36

The Duke of Burgundy addresses the kings of France and England,
hoping that peace will finally come.

Should not in this best garden of the world,
Our fertile France, put up her lovely visage?
Alas, she hath from France too long been chased,
And all her husbandry doth lie on heaps,
Corrupting in it own fertility.
Her vine, the merry cheerer of the heart,
Unprunèd dies . . .

Violet

LOVE'S LABOUR'S LOST ACT 5. SCENE 2. LINE 879

In the play within the play, Spring sings a song.

When daisies pied and violets blue,
    And lady-smocks, all silver-white,
And cuckoo-buds of yellow hue
    Do paint the meadows with delight,
The cuckoo then on every tree
Mocks married men, for thus sings he:
        Cuckoo!
Cuckoo, Cuckoo—O word of fear,
Unpleasing to a married ear.

Walnut

THE TAMING OF THE SHREW ACT 4. SCENE 3. LINE 63

Petruccio derides a hat Katherine desires.

HABERDASHER Here is the cap your worship did bespeak.

PETRUCCIO Why, this was moulded on a porringer—

A velvet dish. Fie, fie, 'tis lewd and filthy.

Why, 'tis a cockle or a walnut-shell,

A knack, a toy, a trick, a baby's cap.

Away with it! Come, let me have a bigger.

Wheat

THE TEMPEST ACT 4. SCENE 1. LINE 60

Iris summons the spirit Ceres.

Ceres, most bounteous lady, thy rich leas

Of wheat, rye, barley, vetches, oats, and peas;

Thy turfy mountains where live nibbling sheep,

And flat meads thatched with stover, them to keep . . .

Willow

HAMLET ACT 4. SCENE 7. LINE 138

Queen Gertrude tells Laertes how his sister, Ophelia, drowned.

There is a willow grows aslant a brook

That shows his hoar leaves in the grassy stream.

Therewith fantastic garlands did she make

Of crow-flowers, nettles, daisies, and long purples,

That liberal shepherds give a grosser name,

But our cold maids do dead men's fingers call them.

There on the pendent boughs her crownet weeds

Clamb'ring to hang, an envious sliver broke,

When down the weedy trophies and herself

Fell in the weeping brook. Her clothes spread wide,

And mermaid-like a while they bore her up;

Which time she chanted snatches of old tunes,

As one incapable of her own distress,

Or like a creature native and endued

Unto that element. But long it could not be

Till that her garments, heavy with their drink,

Pulled the poor wretch from her melodious lay

To muddy death.

Wormwood

LOVE'S LABOUR'S LOST ACT 5. SCENE 2. LINE 833

*Rosaline tells Lord Biron that if he wishes to marry her, he must wait
a year and, to rid himself of his worldly pride, attend the sick.*

To weed this wormwood from your fruitful brain,
And therewithal to win me if you please,
Without the which I am not to be won,
You shall this twelvemonth term from day to day
Visit the speechless sick and still converse
With groaning wretches, and your task shall be
With all the fierce endeavour of your wit
To enforce the painèd impotent to smile.

Yew

ROMEO AND JULIET ACT 5. SCENE 3. LINE 3

Paris instructs the Page.

Under yon yew trees lay thee all along,
Holding thy ear close to the hollow ground.
So shall no foot upon the churchyard tread,
Being loose, unfirm, with digging up of graves,
But thou shalt hear it.

Acknowledgments

I THANK GOD FOR THE OPPORTUNITY TO DO THIS BOOK, AND GIVE MY HEARTFELT THANKS TO MY gorgeous wife, Christine, for all her support throughout. Many thanks to our children, Mark, Micah, and August, for their encouragement. Also to Margaret L. Kaplan, Darilyn L. Carnes, and the team at Abrams for their gifted work.

I am very grateful to those who opened their gardens for photography and shared their enthusiasm for William Shakespeare and the Elizabethan era. Particular thanks to Lord and Lady Salisbury and Robin Harcourt Williams of Hatfield House and Cranborne Manor; the Shakespeare Birthplace Trust and Katie Cain; The Museum of Garden History; Marti Pinnavaia and J. Kosmacher at Vassar College; The Garden Club of Evanston; Strawberry Banke Museum and John Forti; Nancy Moore and Ian Fenwick at UCFV Chilliwack; Christa Robinson; Edwina Von Gal; Richard Norris; David Varnell; Dolores Signori; Robert and Elizabeth Murphy; and William and Mavis Reed.

Thanks to Oxford University Press for the William Shakespeare text taken from *William Shakespeare: The Complete Works*, edited by Stanley Wells and Gary Taylor.

Finally, special gratitude to the Dowager Marchioness of Salisbury for her work in reawakening the public interest in gardens of the Elizabethan era.

Index